Original title:
Socks on a Snowy Morning

Copyright © 2025 Creative Arts Management OÜ
All rights reserved.

Author: Henry Beaumont
ISBN HARDBACK: 978-1-80586-031-0
ISBN PAPERBACK: 978-1-80586-503-2

Cozy Signs in a Frozen Renaissance

In frosty air, a chill does creep,
The dogs beside me start to leap.
With wiggly toes in fluffy wear,
I giggle at how we dance and stare.

The cat, a monarch, claims the throne,
With tiny pads, it claims its zone.
A snowball fight? Oh, what a jest!
But wait—my warm feet, they know best!

Outside, a snowman dons a hat,
While I craft wonders, imagine that!
Flakes fall like laughter from the sky,
As I trip on snow, oh my, oh my!

So here I stand, a comical sight,
With feet like marshmallows, soft and light.
A silly scene of pure delight,
In winter's grip, we laugh and bite!

Serenity Beneath the Icy Canopy

In a world of white, we slip and slide,
Gloves on our hands, we're filled with pride.
Hot cocoa spills, laughter in the air,
It's a frosty ruckus; nobody cares!

Snowflakes dance down from a sky so gray,
Tripping over boots, we tumble and sway.
Chasing our shadows, we giggle and scream,
Winter's a canvas, we paint like a dream.

The Art of Staying Warm

Bundled up tight like a burrito whole,
Scarves wrapped around, oh what a role!
Knitted hats squeeze our brains just right,
Fashion's a joke, but we'll win this fight.

Chasing the chill with a tickle and toast,
Stomping the floor, we're the warmth's proud host.
We huddle together, a giggling crew,
In a world of white, let's paint it in blue.

Winter Whispers in (Fuzzy) Textures

Fuzzy boots shuffle on the glistening ground,
We race through the flakes, laughter all around.
Texture feels lovely between layers thick,
Oh, how we wish for a magic trick!

Slippers parade as we dance in a line,
Sliding and gliding, it's the best of times.
Fuzz balls of warmth waltz in our heads,
Jumps and falls, who cares if it spreads?

Echoes of Light Footsteps

With each soft step, our laughter plays,
Echoing joy through wintery maze.
Fallen snow whispers beneath our feet,
An orchestra of giggles; oh what a treat!

We leap like reindeer, with squeals of delight,
Casting shadows in the pale moonlight.
The world's a stage for our snowy show,
Chasing down magic, just letting it flow.

Sipping Cocoa Amidst Frozen Blankets

A steaming cup warms chilly hands,
Marshmallows float like fluffy bands.
Giggles dance with the frosty air,
Chocolate smiles, banish despair.

Outside, snowflakes play a game,
Each one unique, none the same.
Inside, laughter echoes loud,
Snuggled beneath our snowy shroud.

Dancing Through White Whispers

Fluffy suits and hats so bright,
Snowballs fly, what a sight!
Snowmen wave with carrot noses,
Winter's whimsy never dozes.

Footprints trail through the soft white,
As we twirl, oh what a sight!
Laughter rings in the chilly air,
Winter's magic, we boldly share.

Winter's Cozy Embrace

Tucked in like cookies side by side,
Warmth spreads forth, a joyful tide.
Each sip of warmth tastes like cheer,
Fuzzy feelings, winter's sphere.

Mittens mingle, hats askew,
Chasing dreams that dance anew.
The frosty worlds we can create,
In cozy love, we celebrate.

Flurries Beneath Our Feet

Pitter-patter on the ground,
Tiny flurries twirl around.
With each step, a crunching sound,
Winter's blanket, deep and profound.

Skaters glide with a whoop and cheer,
Laughter echoing far and near.
In the chill, we jump and spin,
With frozen grins, let the fun begin!

Winter's Embrace Wrapped Tight

In the chill, my toes do dance,
Fuzzy things, oh what a chance!
Fluffy beasts upon my feet,
A comical, warm little treat.

Slipping here and sliding there,
Who knew frost could be this rare?
As I wobble, laugh, and spin,
These silly things make me grin!

The Sound of Warmth Cradling Cold

Crunching crisp beneath my feet,
Sound of warmth that can't be beat.
Giggles trail where I go,
Silly sounds in fields of snow.

Flapping fabric, a hushed delight,
Woolly wonders keep me bright.
With every step, my heart does sing,
Oh, the joy that winter brings!

Radiant Reflections in Thick Knit

Brightly colored, patterns sway,
A rainbow dance upon the gray.
They wriggle, jiggle, full of cheer,
As if they know it's time to steer.

Each cozy wrap, a warm embrace,
In this frosty, playful space.
Chasing snowflakes as they fall,
With these knit ones, I stand tall!

Frosted Adventures of the Heart

Little trails that twist and turn,
On this frosty day, I learn.
Motions silly, laughter flows,
Within these twists, adventure grows.

Each frosty leap, each slide, each fall,
These merry moments, I recall.
With playful steps in winter's tune,
I skip along, a joyous boon!

Embracing the Blanket of Cold

Frosty flakes twirl in the air,
I leap like a penguin without a care.
My toes are frozen, but I dance about,
With a smile so wide, I scream and shout.

The world is a canvas, white and bright,
I tumble and giggle, what a delight!
Each step is a squish, oh what a sound,
As the chilly fluff swallows me round.

Joyful Steps Beyond the Window

Through the glass, it glistens and calls,
My rubber boots escape the walls.
I slip and slide, oh what a thrill,
With a hop and a jump, I exert my will.

Neighbors peek out, they laugh and gaze,
Their coffee in hand, in a cozy daze.
I make snow angels with flair and finesse,
In my winter wonder, it's pure happiness!

Whispers of Warmth from Home

Hot cocoa bubbles, a sweet, steamy brew,
But outside I'm wrapped in a chilly debut.
My cheeks are rosy, bright as a rose,
With every snowball, laughter just grows.

Mama shouts, 'Don't track that snow in!'
But I can't resist, it's too much fun to spin.
I dive in the white, leaving trails of glee,
As she shakes her head, I sip my tea.

Enchanted Layers Upon Gentle Snow

Dressed like a marshmallow, I waddle and roll,
Building a queen for my snow-covered goal.
With a carrot for a nose, and a smile of coal,
I envision my kingdom, oh what a stroll!

The fluffy terrain is perfect for play,
Neighbors emerge, joining the fray.
We toss frozen balloons in a friendly fight,
And laugh at the joy of this glittering white!

The Touch of Softness

Fluffy clouds upon my feet,
A cozy hug, oh what a treat!
They dance around with every step,
As laughter echoes, I can't help but prep.

I step outside to greet the chill,
The ground beneath is icy still.
With every squish and little slip,
My grinning face, I cannot grip!

Chasing Flakes in Warm Threads

Little flurries swirl and glide,
While I hop, giggle, and slide!
My feet feel light, I'm full of cheer,
Each frosty leap brings me near.

Oh, the chase of fluffy white,
While bundled up, I'm quite a sight!
With every twist and playful fall,
I catch a snowflake, that's my call!

Milky Paths of Warmth

I march on fluff, a white brigade,
My toes rejoice, they're not afraid!
The winter wonderland is my stage,
While giddy giggles break my cage.

With every twirl, I lift my feet,
A howling laugh, oh what a feat!
In this snowy land, I'm the queen,
In puffy threads, so soft and keen!

Layers of Love on Ice

Wobbling about like a silly bear,
With each small step, I build my flair.
Wrapped in warmth, I scoot and slide,
This frozen playground is my pride.

A fluffy friend joins in the spree,
Together we dance, wild and free!
Fumbling laughter fills the air,
In frosty fun, we have no care!

Cozy Corners in the Chill

In fluffy slippers, I glide with flair,
Chasing my cat, with a leap in the air.
Coffee's steaming, it's spilled on my shirt,
Dishwasher duty—oh joy, what a perk!

I trip on a blanket, it dances around,
The dog gives a chuckle, he thinks I'm a clown.
My mittens are mismatched, who needs any style?
In this cozy chaos, I'll linger a while.

Padding Through a Winter Wonderland

Tiptoe through piles of soft, fluffy snow,
Each step is a whisper, in winter's soft glow.
Mittens on hands, hat lopsided too,
A snowball finds me, and giggles ensue!

The snowman is wobbly, he leans to the right,
With eyes made of buttons, he stares through the night.
I fall on my backside, oh wasn't that fun?
Rolling in snow, now my clothes weigh a ton!

Whimsical Warmth Against the Blue

The laundry pile grows, what a curious sight,
Colors and patterns that dance in delight.
Peeking from baskets, the treasures I find,
In this jumbled world, cozy chaos unwinds.

A chase with my dog, he's wearing my hat,
We tumble and giggle, oh where's my old cat?
Baking some cookies, the flour takes flight,
My kitchen's a circus, but oh what a sight!

Soft Footfalls in Pure White

With laughter as my cloak, I bounce down the hall,
Each footstep's a dance, as I trip and I fall.
A scarf is my sidekick, it wraps 'round my waist,
This joyful parade simply can't go to waste!

The chime of the kettle sings tunes through the air,
While friends bring the snacks—it's a jolly affair.
In hats far too big, we pose for a shot,
In this wintery play, we forget all we've got!

Slippered Steps in Silent White

In fluffy shoes, I dance around,
With every slide, I nearly fall down.
The floor is icy, a winter's lark,
I tiptoe lightly, a comical spark.

The cat looks on, with wide-eyed glee,
As I wobble and hum, feeling so free.
Chasing my balance, I take a twirl,
In my home of magic, it's a winter whirl.

Fuzzy Footprints in Frozen Landscapes

With furry paws, I trot and prance,
Making funny prints, oh what a chance!
I slipped on ice, and then I spun,
My frosty adventure has just begun.

Each step I take, a laughter erupts,
As I bump and slide in snowy abrupts.
The puppy joins with a playful bark,
Together we dance, leaving our mark.

Knit Dreams Beneath Flurries

A twirl of yarn, a knot so tight,
With needles clicking, it's pure delight.
Memo to self, count every stitch,
But here comes the cat, ready to hitch.

She pounces and purrs, a knit ball flies,
In cozy chaos, our laughter rises.
Winter dreams warm in our playful spree,
With tangled yarn, just her and me.

Hearthside Comforts and Frosty Mornings

With woolly wraps, I warm my toes,
In my fortress of blankets, nobody knows.
The coffee brews while I snuggle tight,
Wishing the world was always this bright.

But who spilled cocoa in such a spot?
I'm picking up marshmallows, oh, what a plot!
Laughing at spills with a heart that glows,
In my frosty haven, that's how it goes.

Dayspring in Cozy Layers

When the sun peeks through the gray,
I slip into layers, a parade in play.
My feet are wobblers in fuzzy delight,
They dance with joy, what a glorious sight!

Slippery paths, I glide and I slide,
With each playful step, I'm full of pride.
A puff of feathers keeps me warm,
In this fluffy battle, I choose to charm.

Chasing the cat, oh, what a scene,
He jumps and dodges, quick as a bean.
With a lunging leap, he steals my heart,
In our cozy battle, we're never apart.

So here's to wearing our quirkiest garb,
With morning laughter, we'll never tire.
In bright mismatched colors, how we sway,
In the threads, our joy finds a way!

A Tangle of Threads and Snow

Snowflakes fall like little stars,
But my foot's stuck in a woolly jar.
A tangle of threads, what a goofy plight,
I twist and twirl, a comical sight!

My left foot's giggling, right foot's a tease,
Both want to dance, but they can't quite agree.
In wooly chaos, I leap and I jump,
In this frosty mess, I trip and I bump.

The dog joins in with a howling spree,
Chasing my feet, oh so happily.
I tumble and roll in white billowy fluff,
Proclaiming this morning is silly enough!

So let's make snowmen with mismatched flair,
In a clumsy embrace, we lose all our care.
With a wink to the socks that lead my way,
In tangled laughter, we frolic and sway!

Embers of Warmth on a Frosted Path

On frosty trails, my toes breathe steam,
My goofy mittens are part of the theme.
With mismatched colors, I stomp through the chill,
Creating my own winter wonderland thrill.

Every step feels like a jolly jig,
I swirl and I sway, like a dancing twig.
A stray sock flaps like a cheeky bird,
In this frosted adventure, I'm blissfully absurd!

Puddles of ice make my feet skip high,
Like a playful pup, I leap to the sky.
The snowflakes chuckle at my crazy dance,
Who knew such joy could happen by chance?

So here's to the warmth that keeps us alive,
In our silly antics, we truly thrive.
With each hilarious slip or mishap we make,
We find silly stories that'll surely awake!

Beneath the Snow, Footfalls Rest

Under the blanket of soft silver sheen,
My feet leave tracks with a whimsical keen.
I hop on one foot and then on the other,
Like a silly rabbit, I laugh and I stutter.

The crunch of the frost sends giggles to the sky,
I prance through the drifts as the chilly winds sigh.
My puffy boots twist and twirl with delight,
In the crisp morning air, my heart takes flight!

Caught in a maze, I tumble, I roll,
Hidden beneath is the snowman's soul.
With carrot noses and buttons they grin,
In this clever game, I find a new win.

So let's dance together, a frosty ballet,
With mismatched layers that brighten the day.
In the flurry of fun, my spirit is blessed,
With each sassy footprint, my heart finds rest.

Footprints in Frost

Tiny prints upon the ground,
Each one telling tales profound.
Snowflakes tickle at my toes,
Laughter echoes, warmth grows.

Sliding here and slipping there,
Grumpy snowmen, unaware.
Chasing giggles, slipping fast,
Wonders of the winter cast.

Mittens join the snowy play,
Waving cheer, they lead the way.
Frosty whiskers, all around,
Giggling at the frosty sound.

Every step a wobbly dance,
In this chill, I take my chance.
Frosty fun can't be denied,
With each joyful snowball slide.

Cozy Threads in Winter's Embrace

Threads of warmth, a colorful spree,
Twirling 'round, just like me.
Tangled yarn, oh what a sight,
In my socks, snowflakes take flight.

With every step, a muffled sound,
Woolly wonders all around.
Jumping high with giggles bright,
Chasing snowballs, what a plight!

Puppies pounce with cheer and bark,
Whiskers twitch in frosty park.
Warm toes dance upon the fluff,
Oh, winter, you are such a love!

In my cozy threads I prance,
Join the snow in carefree dance.
Let me twirl in winter's scheme,
Wrapped in wool, I chase the dream.

Warm Treads on Crystal Floors

Glimmers glisten on my feet,
Every step a joyful beat.
With each tread, the frosty gleam,
Warming up a winter dream.

Slippery paths where snowmen grin,
Chasing laughter, let's begin!
I trip, I fall, but all in fun,
Snowflakes sparkling, I'm undone!

Woolly critters all about,
Join the antics, twist and shout.
Snowballs fly, and giggles soar,
Winter's magic, we adore!

Those warm treads find every nook,
In the snow, oh what a look!
With a twirl, I take my flight,
Winter's joy, pure delight!

The Dance of Wool and Snow

Frosty air, a dance begins,
Woolly creatures, little spins.
Twirling round in furry socks,
Winter's laughter, how it rocks!

Sneaky flakes fall from the sky,
Tickling toes as they fly by.
Woolly jumpers join the fun,
Spinning tales till night is done.

A leap, a slip, a giggly fall,
Snowmen laughing, that's the call.
In the cold, we warm our hearts,
With every dance, a new sweet start.

So let us twirl through frosty skies,
Woolen warmth, our true disguise.
Laughter ringing, pure and free,
In this playful winter spree.

The Warmth of Fuzzy Layers

In a drawer, chaos reigns,
Colors clash like silly trains.
I search for pairs, but they sneak away,
Hiding where they surely play.

Stripes and dots, oh what a sight,
Making my feet feel just so right.
They dance around, those playful souls,
Chasing warmth, defying the cold.

A mismatched crew, a quirky lot,
Each one boasts its own hot spot.
Together they laugh, they wiggle gleefully,
In my fuzzy fortress, it's love, you see!

With a wiggle and a happy cheer,
I slip 'em on and feel no fear.
Each step a giggle, a little delight,
Fuzzy layers keep me merry and light.

Toasty Threads in Frosty Air

Frosty breath and chilly skies,
But warmth erupts from fuzzy ties.
A wild mix tangled on the floor,
My feet dive in, then shout for more!

Upstairs, the wind begins to howl,
But down below, I'm free to prowl.
Puppy prints and stomped-out trails,
Dressed for glee, my spirit sails.

The buttons on my knees do squeak,
While splashing snow—oh what a streak!
No absent pairs can dull my fun,
In toasty threads, I'm number one!

Rolling, tumbling, bliss unfolds,
In layered threads, my tale retolds.
Each step a giggle, each twirl a dream,
With frosty air, I'm living the meme!

Nibbles of Comfort

Chilly toes dance on icy floors,
Hopping around, oh, the mischief it explores!
A spicy scent whirls in the breeze,
Wrapped in warmth, oh, what a tease!

Nibbling snacks while I prance,
With cozy threads, I start to dance.
Hot cocoa spills from my happy mug,
As I shimmy with my fuzzy rug.

Each step a merry, silly sound,
As I frolic round and round.
Bits of comfort sprinkle my way,
Like lost socks come out to play!

In a world where laughter glows,
My goofy antics just overflow.
With every twist, my joy expands,
In nibbles of comfort, life is grand!

Gentle Falls of White

Outside, a blanket covers the ground,
While inside my warmth, I've newly found.
Cotton clouds drift from my feet,
As a tangle of colors makes life sweet.

Each gentle fall tickles my toes,
While laughter erupts and joy just flows.
What fun to slip, slide and glide,
In this fluffy world, I take such pride!

The sun peeks in, oh what a scene,
As I bounce in layers of cozy sheen.
Snowflakes swirl and throw a party,
While I twirl and spin, feeling hearty.

Home is a haven, snug and bright,
With gentle falls bringing delight.
A frosty morning, a sprinkle of play,
In my happy realm, I'll always stay!

Padded Steps in a Silent Wonderland

In fluffy clouds beneath my feet,
I skip and slide, oh what a feat!
The chilly floor's a funny game,
With every thud, I squeal my name.

My toes are wiggling, feeling free,
But wait! What's that? Is it just me?
A ghostly shuffle, a chilly dance,
In this frosty room, we've got a chance!

I leap around, a jumbled show,
Each bound reveals my silly glow.
The world outside is dressed in white,
But inside here, I'm pure delight!

What joy in this winter wonderland,
With soft and squishy winter band.
I'll laugh and play, no hint of dread,
Until the evening calls to bed!

Threads of Cheer Amidst the Chill

With bright threads dancing on my feet,
Each step's a giggle, every beat.
A leap, a whirl, I spin around,
As soft and silly joys abound.

The chill outside cannot compete,
With this warm giggle, oh so sweet.
I trip and tumble, how I glide,
In cozy layers, I take pride!

Snow may cover every lane,
But here I bounce without a strain.
I toss the pillows, fake a fall,
In this frosty room, I have it all!

With every move, my spirit's light,
No room for gloom on this fine night.
In cheerful threads, I dance and play,
While winter's chill begins to sway.

Embracing the Icy Glow

I twirl and stomp, my feet so warm,
The chilling air can't break my charm.
I giggle as I glide so tall,
With frosty windows, I've got it all!

The icy floor becomes my stage,
In playful moves, I turn the page.
Each curious step's a comical sight,
As I embrace this winter's light.

I dash around, feeling quite sly,
In this snow globe, I laugh and fly.
Each twist and twirl, I'm full of cheer,
Nothing can dim this joy I wear!

With cushions soft and giggles bright,
I celebrate this frosty night.
To kick up snowflakes, oh what a treat!
Tomorrow's freeze will face my beat!

Magical Layers under Snowflakes

In multiple layers, I bounce with glee,
Each silly step brings joy to me.
The snowflakes outside, they start to fall,
But I'm the champion of this hall!

A flip and flop, I'm light as air,
While snow something might cover everywhere.
The blankets call me, snug and secure,
Yet here I prance, that's for sure!

I leap in joy, not the least shy,
Creating laughter as I fly by.
The cold can't reach this funny scene,
In my bright layers, I'm the queen!

No worries here, just giggles and fun,
With sparkling layers, I've truly won.
When winter's chill tries to spread its charm,
I'll laugh it off, all snug and warm!

Echoes of Toasty Threads in a Winter Wonderland

In my house I trip and slide,
A creature born of fluffy pride.
With mismatched pairs of colors bright,
I dance around in pure delight.

The cat gives me a sideways glance,
As I galumph in this clumsy dance.
Winter's chill won't bring me down,
I'm the jester in this frumpy crown.

The neighbors laugh, they point and tease,
While I juggle wool like autumn leaves.
Who knew a wardrobe could be so grand?
I'm the king with threads unplanned!

Yet with every slip and slipper fall,
My laughter echoes through it all.
For in this chaos, joy I find,
In toasty threads, my heart's aligned.

Warm Embrace of Solitude

In solitude, I waddle round,
The fluffiest beast beneath the mound.
A cup of cocoa by my side,
In layers packed, I choose to hide.

The snowflakes softly drift and twirl,
Outside, the winter wonders swirl.
But here I snuggle, blissfully warm,
A quiet bubble from the storm.

With a scandalous pair of bright magenta,
I revel in my own eventa.
No fashion tips, I toss them far,
Today's style is 'Who needs a car?'

I sip my drink and feel so grand,
As winter wraps me in its hand.
In this embrace of soft delight,
I find my joy in colors bright.

Gentle Comfort in the Frost's Caress

The morning sun peeks through the frost,
While I uncover what I've lost.
A single glove and fuzzy bear,
A tale of warmth beyond compare.

I slip and slide, the floor a field,
With every step, my fate revealed.
But laughter bursts like bubbles pop,
In this cozy, topsy-turvy shop.

Beneath the couch, a rogue one hides,
A wild print that giggles and glides.
I shake my fist, they've pulled a trick,
But no hard feelings—come join the flick!

So here I am, a jester's glee,
With happy wriggles, wild and free.
Embracing all this silly mess,
In frosty air, I find my best.

Warmth Woven into Winter's Silence

In winter's hush, I find my glee,
Wrapped in warmth, oh can't you see?
With knits so crazy, patterns askew,
Each step's an adventure, who knew?

Around the house, it's quite the scene,
Fluffy beasts in shades of green.
I tumble through the snow, a fight,
With every fall, I'm still all right.

The outside world is cold and stark,
While I amuse like clowns in park.
Oh, how the hapless moments glow,
As winter paints a frosty show.

So let them laugh from window panes,
As I wiggle through these woolen lanes.
In every flurry where joy collides,
I find my magic where warmth abides.

Threads of Warmth Amidst the Chill

Bright colors clash with winter's gray,
My toes dance silly, come what may.
Each step's a jump, a playful prance,
In cozy layers, I take a chance.

With stripes and polka dots in tow,
I waddle like a frosty crow.
The world outside is dressed in white,
While I'm a rainbow, pure delight.

The dogs all stare, they do a shake,
As I trip on laces, make a mistake.
But laughs erupt from every fall,
Who knew cozy could cause such a brawl?

In fabric hugs, my heart does sing,
To winter's chill, I offer a fling.
Amidst the frost, I spin and twirl,
A dorky dance, oh what a whirl!

Serene Steps Through Shimmering White

Unruly footprints pepper the scene,
I skip with glee, oh how serene!
With every crunch beneath my feet,
I feel the magic, oh so sweet.

Snowflakes tumble, waltz, and twirl,
While I giggle, a joyful whirl.
A flurry lands upon my nose,
And laughter springs from head to toes.

Chasing snowmen, I prance around,
Creating mischief, laughter resound.
Bundle up, the warmth goes on,
Yet I'm the star in this soft dawn.

Oh winter chill, you cannot find,
A heart so silly, so unrefined.
With every slip, I glide, I roll,
Through shimmering white, I find my soul!

A Tapestry of Warmth in Frost's Grasp

Fuzzy patterns swirl and sway,
As I declare it my parade day.
With each chilly gust that bites,
I wiggle more; what funny sights!

My mismatched threads take center stage,
I'm a hapless, loving winter sage.
A snowball fight, a friendly scene,
Yet I bounce back, all bright and keen.

Giggles erupt from playful friends,
As cold hands meet in joyful blends.
With laughter ringing, we skip about,
On winter's stage, we sing and shout.

Even as frost nips at our cheeks,
The warmth within simply peaks.
In this tapestry of chill and laughter,
I cherish moments long after.

Whispered Hues of a Frozen Dawn

Crimson, green, loud against the frost,
In this color clash, I am not lost.
Each morning's gleam sings to my soul,
A symphony, that's my only goal.

The chilly air brings giggles near,
As I juggle snowballs without a fear.
My winter attire might be a sight,
But joy in misfit feels just right.

With every step, the shivers tease,
Yet laughter dances through the trees.
Oh silly me, all bundled tight,
I trip and tumble, oh what a sight!

In hues of frost, I play so free,
Crafting moments, just wait and see.
Today's a canvas; smiles adorn,
With whispered joy of a frozen morn!

Soft Soles Beneath Winter's Veil

In fuzzy layers, we slide and glide,
With puffy patterns, we shift aside.
Each step a dance, a humored prance,
Before we trip, in this snowy trance.

Laughter echoes through the white,
As we stumble, giggle, and take flight.
The ground so soft, the air so bright,
In cushioned chaos, we delight.

Our toes peek out, a daring feat,
While frosty breezes play with our feet.
Each fluffy sock's a slippery trap,
As we twirl and careen in a wintery nap.

With every slip, a snort does arise,
As drifts entrap us in snowy skies.
We tumble down in heaps of cheer,
Embracing the cold, we have no fear.

Wrapped in Warmth

Cocooned in colors, oh what a sight,
A pile of layers, snug and tight.
We waddle like penguins, awkwardly grand,
As snowflakes dance all over the land.

Each foot a fortress, each toe a guest,
In winter's embrace, we frolic and jest.
The neighbors chuckle, they know we're near,
With mismatched patterns and plenty of cheer.

Our laughter rings, a delightful tune,
As we trip through the snow, under the moon.
Wrapped in warmth, with hearts so light,
We make merry mischief on this snowy night.

A tumble here, a spin so wide,
Our valiant efforts serve as our pride.
In kitschy attire, we run with glee,
Some woolly nonsense, we are all free!

Chasing Snowflakes

We dash and dart, beneath the flakes,
Like joyful puppies with cake-filled stakes.
Arms flailing, laughter takes the air,
As we leap through drifts without a care.

We chase the heavens, hearts on fire,
With every twirl, we climb higher.
But oh, the tumble, the glorious fall,
With snowy splats, we embrace it all.

A fluffy cloud, a pile of white,
We fashion snowballs, ready to fight.
But wait! What's this? A slip and slide,
With sassy grins, we can't confide.

In this frozen playground, we're wild and bold,
With stories unfolding as memories unfold.
Each gust of laughter, each snowy spree,
In chase of the flakes, we find pure glee.

Gentle Wanderings on White Silence

In serene silence, we venture today,
On billowy waves of fluffy play.
Each step whispers, soft as a dream,
Where sunlight glimmers, and snowflakes gleam.

We tiptoe lightly, a careful spree,
Yet giggles bubble, so carefree.
A hop, a skip, a skip and stomp,
In this winter wonder, we joyously romp.

The chill bites gentle, a playful tease,
Yet warmth abounds, with laughter that frees.
We scuffle and shuffle, making our way,
In winter's charm, we choose to stay.

From frosty bobbles to wild snowball fights,
We twirl through the snow till the day turns to night.
In this white wonder, we lose all sense,
Dancing with frost, so merry and dense.

Nature's Quilt and the Warmth Within

The ground is layered, a quilt of white,
Each patch a story, as day turns night.
With patches of laughter and stitches of fun,
We prance through the drifts till the day is done.

Our feet poke through, beneath the seams,
Inventing new games and giggly schemes.
A hop on the surface, a slide right down,
In this frosty fortress, we wear our crown.

Each chuckle a thread, each snowflake a share,
A tapestry woven with winter's flair.
In mittens and boots, we twirl and whirl,
Nature's quilt wraps us in a soft swirl.

So here we gather, with joy on display,
Warmth in our hearts, come what may.
With silly adventures in every spin,
We embrace the chill and the warmth within.

Flakes Dance Around the Cozy Glow

Flakes fall down, a fluttering show,
A cozy glow on the ground below.
Laughter spills from a frosty smile,
As we slip and slide just for a while.

Hot cocoa spills on a chair too small,
Warmed by giggles, we start to sprawl.
The antics begin as we tumble around,
With a fluffy friend who can't stay on the ground.

Chasing snowmen, their noses of coal,
Warming up with some pie, that's our goal.
A snowball fight, oh what a sight!
We laugh 'til we cry, hearts feeling light.

Through snowflakes and warmth, the fun never ends,
With cozy connections and good-hearted friends.
Every slip, every slide, a new kind of cheer,
In this winter wonder, we hold very dear.

Where Wool Meets Snow's Gentle Touch

Woolly wonders on a chilly spree,
Whirls of white prepare to set us free.
Each step we take is a squishy delight,
As we hop and skip in the frosty white.

Marshmallow dreams on this fluffy ground,
With every misstep, more laughter found.
Rolling around in a soft, snowy hug,
As we cuddle close and give warmth a tug.

Next, a snow angel, though lopsided sideways,
With giggles erupting in whimsical ways.
Snug in our layers, we frolic and play,
Turning winter's chill into joyful ballet.

When snowflakes twirl, we all feel alive,
In laughter and warmth, the spirit will thrive.
WIth wool wrapped cozily against winter's pinch,
We conquer the cold with every silly flinch.

Feeling at Home Among the Cold

Amongst the cold, we find our cheer,
Noses red, but our hearts so near.
Slipping through puddles of snowy delight,
Woven together, we dance through the night.

With mittens clashing, we make a parade,
Footprints zig-zag like a wild charade.
In woolly layers, we come to explore,
Turning mundane into the tales we adore.

Wobbly snowmen stand straight with pride,
While we roll and tumble, oh what a ride!
Snowflakes land on our cheeks like a kiss,
Each chilly moment is a memory we'd miss.

At home in the cold, here we all roam,
Spreading warm laughter wherever we comb.
In each frosty chuckle, love's echoes entwine,
Reveling in friendship, cold doesn't confine.

Winter's Gentle Tapestry

In a tapestry woven of fluffy white,
We spin around, losing track of the night.
Each step an adventure, we giggle aloud,
As we journey through winter, feeling enshrouded.

The chill's just a tease, we push through the freeze,
Creating snow forts—oh, where's the easiest squeeze?
With silly whispers and toes that squish,
A playful dance as we jump, spin, and swish.

Under the glow of soft wintry light,
With laughter and warmth, everything feels right.
A flurry of fun fills the whirling air,
As snowflakes giggle, joining our flair.

In a cozy cocoon, while chilly winds blow,
We find joy in our antics, a wondrous show.
With hearts intertwined in this joyful spree,
Winter's sweet magic is wild and carefree.

Embracing Chill with Fibered Fleece

On frigid floors I tiptoe fast,
My trusted foot warmers hold me steadfast.
With every step, I slip and slide,
A frosty dance, oh, what a ride!

Around the room, I zig and zag,
In cozy layers, I'm quite the brag.
I twirl and spin, my feet do cheer,
As my furry friends all draw near.

Outside the window, flakes do fall,
Inside, I'm bouncing, loving it all.
A chilly morn turned into glee,
Who knew winter could be so free?

With cups of cocoa and warm delight,
I giggle at my fuzzy fight.
For in this house of warmth and cheer,
I embrace the cold, with a grin ear to ear.

Morning's Breath on Cold Canvas

The world outside wears glistening white,
While inside here, I feel just right.
Each step I take is a little laugh,
As if I'm practicing a silly craft.

With fluffy threads that hug my toes,
I prance around, let nothing cause woes.
The floor's a tundra, yet I glide,
In playful leaps, I take great pride.

Snowflakes whirling, a waltz they make,
But here I am, a joyous quake.
My footsies dance, a joyous song,
In my fibered fortress, I belong.

So let the chilly winds blow strong,
My heart is light, my spirit's song.
In a world of white, oh how I play,
With warmth and cheer, I seize the day.

Textured Journeys Across Icebound Meadows

With every step, a crunch and crack,
The frosty ground has me on track.
Clumsy kitty joins the fun,
We're both unsure of what's to come!

A tumble here, a giggle there,
Two silly souls, without a care.
In mismatched warmth, we explore our way,
Through winter's canvas, we dance and sway.

Beyond the porch, the world is bright,
But I prefer the cozy sight.
With fuzzy warmth wrapped round my feet,
This is the morning I can't be beat.

So bring on winter, all its flair,
With fibered friends, I've got my pair.
In mischief and joy, we'll laugh and play,
A textured journey on this chilly day.

The Sweet Comfort of Woolly Retreats

When dawn appears, the air is crisp,
I wriggle my toes, a little lisp.
With clouds of fluff to wrap me tight,
I feel like jumping with pure delight.

A frosty breeze gives me a tease,
But cozy layers bring me to ease.
With every giggle, I bounce around,
In my woolly haven, joy is found.

Oh, out the door, the cold does call,
But here inside, I'll never fall.
Adventures wait beyond the glass,
But first, in warmth, I'll sip and amass.

So here I stay, in furry bliss,
Each chilly moment too good to miss.
With laughter swirling in this retreat,
In comfy confines, life feels sweet.

Adventures in Wool

In a drawer hidden from sight,
Lies a pair that brings delight.
Colors clash, oh what a scene,
Dancing patterns, bright and keen.

One's all stripes, the other's spots,
Mix 'em up, and laugh a lot!
Off to battle the frosty breeze,
Who knew warmth could hold such tease?

With every step, a silly squish,
Letting out a funny wish.
Woolly caps toss on my head,
In this fashion, I'm well-read!

Wandering through the snowy delight,
With garments loud, a joyful sight.
Each little slip, a giggly gasp,
Oh, the joy of a cozy clasp!

A Dance with Cold

Twirl and spin in frozen air,
With gleeful steps, without a care.
My fluffy friends, they swirl and sway,
In mismatched splendor, come what may.

A frosty breeze gives a cheeky poke,
I leap and dodge—oh, what a joke!
Slippery paths make me glide and slide,
On winter's stage, I take such pride.

Neighbors peek from windows wide,
At my tumbles, they laugh and bide.
Call me clumsy, call me bold,
In this game of fun and cold.

Oh to be a child once more,
With every slip, I dance and soar.
Embracing laughter, a light indeed,
In this frozen world, I take the lead!

Snuggled In Against the Chill

When frost bites at my furry feet,
I find my fortress, soft and neat.
Layer upon layer, a cozy mess,
A fashion choice? Oh, I confess!

Staying in, I hear the snow,
They tumble down, so soft and slow.
With steaming cocoa and a grin,
This woolly joy is where I've been.

Neighbors slide by, so sleek and spry,
While I'm wrapped up and oh so shy.
Watching their dance from my warm nest,
Missing out? No, I'm quite blessed!

What fun it is to laugh alone,
While outside plays this chilly drone.
With patterns bold, I twiddle my toes,
Bubble socks without any woes!

Whispers of Winter Warmth

In a quiet room, the frost won't bite,
With happy fabrics, all snug and right.
Woolly whispers wrap me tight,
As snowfall blankets the world in white.

Giggles echo as I hop around,
Wools and patterns, so much fun found!
Mismatched colors flaring bright,
A quirky parade of warm delight.

Through the window, snowflakes tease,
Their icy dances, a frosty breeze.
While I'm here, all snug within,
My laughter flows, let the fun begin!

Each little slip, a tale to weave,
In this cozy dream, I believe.
Oh winter, such a frosty friend,
With warm woolly hugs, does it ever end?

Wrapped in A Warm Embrace

In a pile of fluff, they bide their time,
Like sneaky ninjas caught in a mime.
They slip and slide, a wobbly dance,
Each leap and twirl, a silly chance.

Colors collide in a playful spree,
One red, one blue, oh where could they be?
Like mismatched gloves, they laugh and tease,
Hiding away, stirring up unease.

Their cotton hearts, they knit and weave,
In winter's chill, they won't deceive.
With warmth and joy, they cozy in
A tangled hug, where giggles begin.

A pair distinct, yet together they climb,
In a world of snow, oh so sublime.
Tickling toes, in chilly embrace,
Each layer a story, a comedic space.

Delicate Choreography of Threads

In the morning light, they start to prank,
With threads entwined, they form a flank.
A ballet of fabric in the frosty air,
Twisting and tangling without a care.

One leaps left, the other spins right,
In this fashion battle, what a sight!
A whirl of colors, they jive and giggle,
With each little twist, they dance and wiggle.

They hunt for warmth in a chilly muse,
But slip on the floor, what a comical ruse!
A tumble and roll, they land with grace,
These lively layers, an epic embrace.

With every wriggle, their canvas grows,
A patchwork quilt of wintery woes.
They snicker together, a cheerful array,
A frosted comedy that brightens the day.

A Soft Journey Through Snow

In the winter's grip, they take to the street,
Padded with laughter, oh what a treat!
Each tiny footstep a printable sound,
As they dance through the drifts that blanket the ground.

They plunge and plop, a playful parade,
Each jump a splash, a frosty charade.
Colors collide, like a candy cane swirl,
In this snowy world, they giggle and twirl.

With every misstep, a chuckle escapes,
They tumble and roll, doing funny shapes.
Their puffy forms catch flakes in their flight,
Wearing snowflakes like crowns, what a delight!

In chilly exploits, they surely will tread,
Crafting new stories as they're comfortably led.
A soft journey on winter's canvas expanse,
Where laughter and joy lead the silly dance.

Playful Stitches in Frosted Adventures

From the closet, they leap, full of cheer,
Like little soldiers marching, oh so clear.
In a frosty land, they play and compete,
Having a blast, with warm, tender feet.

Each stitch a giggle, each seam a song,
Journeying forth, where the brave belong.
With bellies of fluff, they dash 'round the tree,
In this winter scene, they are wild and free.

They twirl through the air, like socks on a spree,
Mischievous threads invite jubilee.
Spinning and jumping, a whimsical sight,
In this frozen realm, everything feels right.

When night falls down, they rest with a grin,
Their fluffy dreams of the day dance within.
In this quilt of warmth, they find their parade,
In playful mischief, true joy is made.

Symphony of Warmth Amidst the Freeze

Amidst winter's chill, they gather in pairs,
A symphony struck through giggles and glares.
Waves of cotton, a colorful band,
Performing a show where the frost meets the hand.

They shuffle and shake, a comical tune,
Bouncing and laughing while sporting a swoon.
With each little hop, they sway in delight,
As snowflakes descend from the starry night.

Their cozy embrace makes snug as a bug,
Recording each moment, a warmth-filled hug.
In the silent embrace of the snowfall below,
These playful dancers put on quite a show.

Through laughter and joy, this troupe does unite,
In a world turned frosty, they spread delight.
With threads of affection and a wiggle or two,
They remind us of fun in everything we do.

Gentle Hues of a Winter's Tale

In fuzzy foot attire so bright,
We dance and twirl with glee tonight.
Each pair a clash, a wild display,
Who knew winter could be so gay?

With stripes and polka dots galore,
They wiggle, squirm across the floor.
A perfect match? Oh what a joke!
They trip and fall, we laugh and poke.

Hot cocoa waits, we're feeling bold,
But look, there's frost upon the cold.
Our feet so warm, the world a chill,
In crazy gear, we have our thrill.

So grab a friend, and join the show,
In colorful warmth, let laughter flow.
Together we'll conquer through this freeze,
In mismatched pairs, with ample cheese!

Knit Dreams Under Gray Skies

Each stitch a tale of wooly cheer,
In colors bright that draw us near.
But oh! Beware the laundry day,
The dryer gobbles what we say!

Here's one that vanished, snapping tight,
Who knew it'd wander off tonight?
A cheeky sock, it slipped away,
To join a tour of playful play.

We search beneath the couch, the chair,
Our furry friends just give a stare.
A quest for mates is what we seek,
In jolly colors, laughter's peak.

So here's to whimsy, life's delight,
As mismatched footies take their flight.
In gray skies dull, we wear a grin,
For laughter's warmth, we always win.

The Note of Warmth and Chill

Crisp mornings greet our happy feet,
In cozy layers, warmth's a treat.
But style, you ask? It's quite a craze,
With colors dancing, bold displays!

The left one's blue, the right is red,
With silly prints, they make us spread.
A giggle here, a chuckle there,
In winter wear, we have a flair!

As neighbors peek out, puzzled looks,
They laugh at our unplanned hook.
In vibrant shades and patterns loud,
We strut around, so wildly proud.

So shake those toes in frisky fun,
In mismatched warmth, we've surely won!
As chilly winds blow through the lane,
Our spirit shines, through joy and pain!

Delicately Adorned in Winter's Fashion

Adventures call beneath the frost,
In funny footwear, we're never lost.
With patterns bold and colors bright,
We slip and slide, what pure delight!

Each daring leap, there goes a pair,
It journeys off, no one to care.
A sock escapes, it frolics free,
Joining a dance, oh can't you see?

With frosty air and laughter loud,
We prance about, we're oh so proud.
Woolly friends from every nook,
Blend into tricks, a comic book!

So let us toast to warmth and fun,
In quirky garb, our race is run.
Through snowy scrambles, fun unfolds,
In knitwear magic, life beholds!

Frosty Mornings and Cozy Evenings

Chilled toes dance in fluff so bright,
The floor's a shock, oh what a fright!
Bundled tight, we slip and slide,
With giggles echoing, we bide our stride.

Hot cocoa sips on cushioned chairs,
Socks strewn about, without a care.
Laughter erupts with each warm sip,
As chilly breezes give us a grip.

Rug's a monster munching on our feet,
Making every step, oh what a feat!
We dive and dodge in a fabric sea,
As if a circus, wild and free.

The sun peeks in, brightening the scene,
Ready for mischief, oh so keen!
With our warm shields, we boldly dare,
To tangle with fluff, and play with air.

Laughter Among White Coverings

In cotton clouds, we find our grace,
Unexpected tumbles, a funny embrace.
With every wrong step, chuckles arise,
As we spread laughter beneath pale skies.

Twisting and turning, like playful spins,
Catching each other as the fun begins.
Snowflakes twirl around our heads,
Making us giggle, oh so widespread!

The wind whispers secrets, a playful tease,
While our footsie fights warm hearts with ease.
Creeping in shadows of snowy delight,
Our joyful shuffles bring warmth to the night.

Frozen toes tapping a playful beat,
As if the world sings beneath our feet.
We jester and jive under blankets bright,
Finding our joy in the chilly twilight.

Treading Lightly in the Cold

With every cautious step, a sudden slide,
As we wobble and giggle, oh what a ride!
The carpet's a monster, it tries to consume,
While we dissolve into laughter's bloom.

Chasing each other with goofy jests,
Making the most of our cozy vests.
The frosty air tickles, we squeal and spin,
With a hop and a skip, the chaos begins!

Warm toes sneak under the blanket's fold,
Where stories and giggles fervently unfold.
A fortress of warmth against winter's bite,
We reign supreme in our fabric delight.

With bright dreams dancing in slumber's embrace,
We drift off together, a warm, happy place.
In the stillness, whispers of fun will stay,
Until the next frosty dawn to play!

Gentle Warmth in a Frosty Realm

In cozy realms where laughter flows,
With playful jabs and friendly throws.
A frosty morning, yet spirits soar,
As we take on winter with a hearty roar.

Beneath layers thick, we slip and roll,
Tumble and giggle, each acting the fool.
With mischief brewing in every nook,
We weave our tales, like a storybook.

The chilly air steals a breath or two,
But warmth from within begins to renew.
With silly prances, the fun has no end,
As laughter's our warmth, our closest friend.

When evening arrives, in laughter we bask,
Wrapped in the glow, what a joyful task!
With hearts wide open, we'll chase away cold,
In our frosty world, where tales are told.

Cherished Moments in Frosty Air

Fumbling fingers, fluffy feet,
In a cozy place, we greet.
With mischief brewing in our souls,
We giggle as the warm tea rolls.

Slipping, sliding, what a race,
Mismatched colors give a chase.
Laughter fills the icy morn,
As cozy chaos there is born.

Fluffy Companions in a White Wonderland

Dressed for battle—what a sight!
With puffs and plops, we take flight.
A tumble here, a roll in fun,
Bright hues twirl under the sun.

Chasing snowflakes, with warm glee,
Our fluffy friends dance wild and free.
In this silly, frosty show,
We leap and flip in the deep snow.

Daring Dances with the Chill

With every shiver, giggles grow,
Clumsy waltzes, to and fro.
Twirling round, I lose my shoes,
But slip and slide is all we choose.

Caught in frosty, silly spins,
Laughter erupts as the fun begins.
Daring dips, we tumble low,
Winter's rhythm steals the show.

Toasty Tango in a Winter Scene

A jolly jig on frosty ground,
With every tumble, joy is found.
Fuzzy layers, quite a sight,
In our dance, we take flight.

With a twist, then a hop,
Snowflakes swirl, we never stop.
As warmth embraces every cheek,
Our laughter echoes, light and sleek.

Threads of Joy in Winter's Bite

On frosty floors, my toes do prance,
In fuzzy wraps, I take my chance.
The chilly air may try to gnaw,
But I've got warmth—just look at my paw!

The cat just stares, eyes all aglow,
As I attempt a comic toe show.
The snowflakes dance, pure white and bright,
While I create my own delight!

Slipping, sliding, what a sight!
With cotton fluff, I own the night.
My winter attire, a cozy spree,
Each step is giggles, each twirl is glee!

Oh, winter winds can howl and cry,
But here I am, just passing by.
With playful leaps and hearty cheer,
I conquer cold with no fear near!

Comfort in Every Stitch

Wrapped in threads like a warm embrace,
Each little pattern, my favorite place.
A maze of colors on my feet,
March with me, beat by beat!

When snowflakes tumble, I break out wide,
In my snuggly gear, I take a ride.
The world may freeze, but I'll just grin,
Each daring step sparks joy within.

Oh, how the dog looks with wide-eyed surprise,
As I leap around in my woolly guise.
With every shuffle on icy ground,
Laughter echoes, a festive sound!

Though winter's sting may seek to bite,
I'll dance around through sun and night.
For worry's not what stitches weave,
Just comfort found, I dare believe!

Happy Feet in a Crystal World

I bounce along through drifts so deep,
With twinkling toes, my joy I keep.
Each icy patch, a thrilling chance,
To break into a silly dance!

The snowman winks with a carrot nose,
As I stumble on, my laughter flows.
The chilly breeze laughs just like me,
I'm only silly; you'll agree!

My toasty toes take center stage,
When winter calls, I disengage!
With every step and flake that falls,
I query how I can have it all!

Giggles burst from tip to heel,
Around each corner, joy to steal.
In this crystal realm, I twirl with glee,
Happy feet forever free!

Steps Through a Winter Dream

With every step, I leave a trace,
In a winter wonderland, I find my place.
These little boots may make me slide,
But, oh, the laughs I can't abide!

The world is white, a frosty scene,
I frolic fast, feeling like a queen.
Each crunch and crackle, a funny song,
In my fluffy gear, I glide along!

Snowflakes twirl like confetti bright,
While I juggle balance—a comical sight!
The streetlamp nods, it knows the score,
Winter fun is hard to ignore!

So here I dance, a joyful tease,
With chilly winds, I take my ease.
In every playful, snowy gleam,
I leap through life—a winter dream!

www.ingramcontent.com/pod-product-compliance
Lightning Source LLC
Chambersburg PA
CBHW070312120526
44590CB00017B/2640